Made for you
you
SPRING

SEASONAL RECIPES FOR GIFTS AND CELEBRATIONS

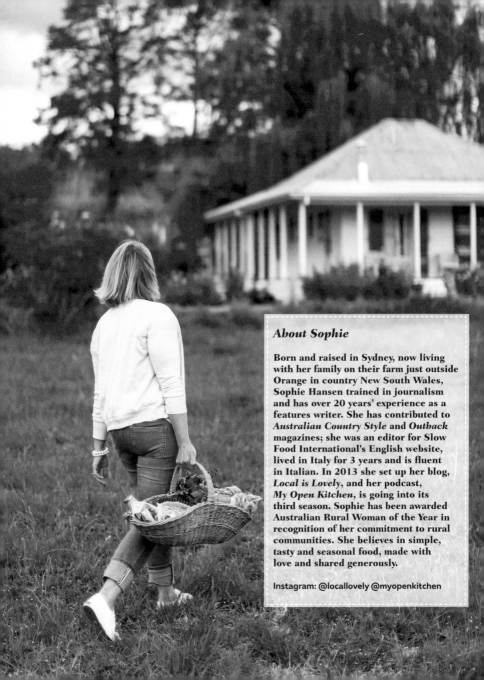

About Sophie

Born and raised in Sydney, now living with her family on their farm just outside Orange in country New South Wales, Sophie Hansen trained in journalism and has over 20 years' experience as a features writer. She has contributed to *Australian Country Style* and *Outback* magazines; she was an editor for Slow Food International's English website, lived in Italy for 3 years and is fluent in Italian. In 2013 she set up her blog, *Local is Lovely*, and her podcast, *My Open Kitchen*, is going into its third season. Sophie has been awarded Australian Rural Woman of the Year in recognition of her commitment to rural communities. She believes in simple, tasty and seasonal food, made with love and shared generously.

Instagram: @locallovely @myopenkitchen

Made for you
SPRING

SEASONAL RECIPES FOR GIFTS
AND CELEBRATIONS

Make ~ Wrap ~ Deliver

Sophie Hansen

murdoch books
Sydney | London

CONTENTS

Food for thought

In happy times and sad, when there are mouths to feed but no energy or time to cook, when recovering or recalibrating… food is always the answer. And while I know that a chicken pie can't fix what's broken, it might just part the clouds a little, and that's something.

Yes, we all know this – that the very best way to show someone how much you care is to cook for them. By doing this, you are saying not only do you care that they are eating well, but also that they are worth your time. You are saying 'I set aside a Saturday morning to bake and wrap and deliver this cake to you because I love you and want you to know and taste that'.

But sometimes inspiration for just what to cook can be elusive, and the whole thing feels a bit hard. Here's where my little book comes in! *Made For You* is a collection of recipes that celebrate not only the welcome arrival of spring, but also the generous, loving act of cooking for people.

This book itself was born of another birth. When we brought our daughter Alice home from hospital, 12 years ago, there was a basket waiting for us by the front door. That basket contained some braised lamb shanks, a cake, a bunch of flowers and a bottle of wine. The gesture bowled me over – not only had that person driven 30 minutes out of town to our farm and front door, she had done so when she knew we wouldn't be home yet (considerate, don't you think, as bringing baby home for the first time isn't a time for entertaining others!) and the gift itself meant that our first few dinners as a brand-new family were sorted. Generosity and love on so many levels.

Ever since that day, I've tried to reciprocate and take care packages to friends in need of nourishing, bolstering, thanking, cheering or just a little bit of looking after.

The following pages are full of the kinds of things I make and share once winter breaks and gives way to spring. All made and photographed on or around our farm in country Australia, there are bright and healthy smoothies, soothing soups, *THE* chicken pie (a labour of love but so very worth it and loved by all), tarts, muffins, picnic ideas and afternoon tea treats.

Most of the recipes can and should be doubled (so you are stocking your own fridge and pantry at the same time - win-win!). They are easy to make, do not ask for expensive ingredients and, most important of all, taste delicious. I hope that they inspire you to put aside a few hours this weekend, to play some good music and make a pie, cake, jar of biscuits or batch of soup for someone who needs a little bit of extra love. Maybe for yourself, maybe for a friend – preferably both.

Packing up your care parcels

While your friends and family will always be grateful for any care package or gift of food you make for them, please don't expect your expensive containers to boomerang right back to you. If they are going through a difficult time, washing and dropping back other people's Tupperware will be at the very bottom of their long list of obligations. So please, lower your expectations and instead of giving a casserole or cake in a container you'd like to see again, maybe use an old pre-loved container or make your own wrapping. Another option is to head to your local opportunity store and find a casserole dish for a few dollars, wash it up and hand it on full of goodness.

And if you're going to all that effort to make something delicious, why not make it look as gorgeous as possible, too? I have a basket in the pantry where I keep my nice paper, cards, pens, ribbons, scissors and muslins. So when a cake or care package is heading out the door, it's easy to find what I need to wrap it up beautifully. Wrap warm cakes in muslin (so they can still breathe) or in baking paper and tie with twine. Give nuts or biscuits in a glass jar tied with ribbon. Take some inspiration from the Japanese art of furoshiki and use old scraps of fabric to wrap and turn anything from loaves of bread to ugly plastic containers into gorgeous home-made gifts.

Practical tips for giving food

There are a few general rules of thumb to be aware of here so the care packages you give don't run any chance of making anyone sick (that would be the polar opposite of what we are trying to do here!). Always wash your hands before cooking and be aware of safe temperatures and storage times. Once cooked, cool food on the bench until steam stops rising, then place in the fridge. Don't let food cool completely on the bench. And don't put hot food straight in the freezer – cool it in the fridge first. Cooked food can generally be safely stored in the fridge for 3 to 4 days only.

To freeze casseroles, divide them into servings of a size that suits your family or the family they are heading to, then place in freezer-safe containers or bags, label with the name of the dish and the date and freeze for 2 to 3 months. Avoid freezer burn by using good thick, resealable bags or quality containers and leave a couple of centimetres at the top of the bag or container to allow for the food to expand when frozen. The best and safest place to thaw frozen food is in the fridge. Always transport food packed in a cool box or insulated bag surrounded with plenty of ice packs.

Watercolour gift tags

I'm not at all arty but have recently begun to play around with little line drawings coloured in with watercolour paints. If you start small and slow, anyone can draw and/or paint, even a tiny little bit.

And after spending most days at a computer or rushing around in the kitchen, I rather love pulling out my little pot of watercolour paints after dinner and doing up cute labels for preserves, salts and other gifts. Please have a go – it's a very un-scary way to be creative, and watercolour paints are so very forgiving so you can't go wrong.

Beeswax food wraps

These wraps have become popular in recent years as a smart, eco-friendly alternative to plastic wrap. And while you can find them in shops, beeswax wraps are usually fairly expensive. But here's the good news: they're super cheap and easy to make. So grab some fabric (an old shirt or pillowcase) and make up a bunch of wraps to give away as presents and/or wrap gifts, sandwiches for school lunches, cover bowls of leftovers and so on.

You'll need 200 g (7 oz) solid beeswax (find it online or in speciality stores), 1 tablespoon olive oil, pinking shears, an old paintbrush, baking paper, a few baking trays and 6–8 fabric rectangles (they'll need to fit on your baking trays, so use that as a size guide).

Preheat the oven to 150°C (300°F). Line your baking trays with baking paper and place a piece of fabric on each. Melt the beeswax in a glass bowl over a pan of simmering water, stir in the oil, then brush it over the fabric. Pop in the oven for a few minutes, then brush again so the wax evenly and lightly covers the fabric. Hang on a clothesline to dry and they're ready to use. Wash beeswax wraps in lukewarm water, never in the dishwasher! If you find them a bit stiff, just work with your hands for a minute until the warmth makes them pliable.

Spring nourish basket

Coconut and lemongrass broth with zucchini 'noodles' ~ Pistachio, cardamom and rose balls
Bright and zingy green smoothie ~ Strawberry, almond and cardamom smoothie ~ Fresh almond milk

I would have loved to find this basket of goodies on arriving home from
hospital with a newborn. In fact, I'm sure anyone needing a little gentle nourishment
would be delighted to receive it. The noodle broth provides a soothing, healthy dinner,
while the smoothies and bliss balls will sort out any hunger pangs. For an even
more perfect package, add a bag of granola (page 31) and a parcel of
Golden syrup biscuits (page 52).

Coconut and lemongrass broth with zucchini 'noodles'

COCONUT AND LEMONGRASS BROTH WITH ZUCCHINI 'NOODLES'

This simple, super-tasty broth is an excellent marriage of comfort and zing, the creamy coconut milk bringing the former and the zippy aromatics the latter. It's also great for those trendy 'soup jar' situations that are all over Pinterest and an excellent 'not-sad desk lunch'.

1 bunch coriander (cilantro)
4 lemongrass stems
2 x 400 ml (14 fl oz) tins coconut milk
4 cm (1½ inch) piece ginger, peeled and finely chopped
2 French shallots, finely diced
1 bird's eye chilli, halved lengthways
1 tsp palm sugar (jaggery)
8 kaffir lime leaves
Juice of 3 limes, plus extra lime wedges to serve
2 Tbsp tamari or soy sauce
2 zucchini (courgettes)
100 g (3½ oz) vermicelli noodles, cooked according to packet instructions
1 handful greens (shredded kale, roughly chopped English spinach, bok choy, etc.)

Chop off the coriander roots and rinse off any grit. Toss the stalks in the compost or chook bin and reserve the leaves. Trim the tops and bottoms off the lemongrass stems and bruise each stem with the flat side of your knife to release as much of the beautiful flavour as possible.

Pour the coconut milk into a saucepan and add the coriander roots, lemongrass, ginger, shallots, chilli and palm sugar. Crush the lime leaves in your palm to release the flavour, and add to the pan. Bring to a gentle boil, then reduce the heat to low and simmer for 25 minutes.

Strain the broth and discard the aromatics. Stir in 1 cup (250 ml) water, the lime juice and tamari. Check the flavour – you want a good balance of sweet, sour and salty.

To prepare the zucchini noodles, if you have a spiraliser, now is the time to drag it out of the back of the cupboard. Otherwise a julienne peeler or a regular sharp knife will do the job nicely.

If serving immediately, pour the hot coconut broth over the zucchini and vermicelli noodles and throw a few of the greens into each bowl. Serve with the reserved coriander leaves and an extra squeeze of lime.

To prepare for later, pour the coconut broth into a thermos or jar and place the noodles and greens in another container. To serve, reheat the broth if necessary and pour it over the noodles and greens.

SERVES 2

This makes an easy lunch or dinner for a friend in need of TLC.

PISTACHIO, CARDAMOM AND ROSE BALLS

'Bliss balls' and the like are super popular these days, and for good reason – they are filling, delicious, easy to make and last well. And while some can be a bit dense and rubbery, these fragrant little numbers are neither. You could swap the LSA mix with almond meal and leave off the chocolate if you're being a bit more health conscious.

½ cup (70 g) pistachios
½ cup (60 g) LSA mix
8 dates, pitted
1 Tbsp honey
1 tsp vanilla bean paste
1 tsp rosewater
¼ tsp ground toasted cardamom (page 75)
A generous pinch of sea salt, plus extra to serve
½ cup (75 g) roughly chopped white chocolate
Edible flowers, to garnish (optional)

Combine all the ingredients (except the chocolate and flowers) in a food processor or high-powered blender. Blend to a rough, sticky paste.

With damp hands, roll the mixture into 10 to 12 balls about the size of a walnut shell. Pop in the fridge to cool and firm up for at least 15 minutes.

Melt the white chocolate in a bowl over a saucepan of simmering water. Drizzle the chocolate over each ball, sprinkle with a few edible flowers and a little more sea salt and return to the fridge for the chocolate to set.

MAKES 10–12

BRIGHT AND ZINGY GREEN SMOOTHIE

1 small handful kale or English spinach
1 ripe banana (preferably frozen)
1 kiwifruit, peeled
½ avocado, stone removed
3 dates, pitted
3 or 4 mint leaves
1 Tbsp chia seeds
1 cup (250 ml) coconut water or plant milk of your choice
Juice of 1 lime
A few ice cubes

Mix all the ingredients in a high-powered blender until smooth.

SERVES 1

We often forget about breakfast when sending and giving food to friends, but when you're feeling a bit fragile or exhausted, having something nutritious, easy and filling ready to go is an enormous help. When you're tied up with a new baby or recovering from an illness or operation, you don't always have the ingredients or time to put them together. These smoothies will keep in the fridge for up to 2 days. Just give them a good shake before drinking, and keep them cool while transporting.

STRAWBERRY, ALMOND AND CARDAMOM SMOOTHIE

6 large strawberries
¼ tsp ground toasted cardamom (page 75)
1 tsp grated fresh ginger
3 dates, pitted
A pinch of sea salt
1 cup (250 ml) fresh almond milk (see recipe, right) or store-bought
A few ice cubes
Honey, to taste

Mix all the ingredients in a high-powered blender until smooth. Sweeten to taste with a little honey (although I find if the strawberries are nice and sweet you don't need to).

NOTE
You could make this creamy smoothie with regular milk or any other nut milk, but I do especially love it with freshly made almond milk.

SERVES 1

FRESH ALMOND MILK

Soak 1 cup (160 g) raw almonds overnight in cold water. Drain and tip into a high-powered blender along with 1 cup (250 ml) water and a pinch of sea salt and blitz for 30 seconds or until you have a smooth paste. Add 2 cups (500 ml) water and 2 pitted dates and blitz for 1 minute. Grab a piece of muslin (or a nut milk bag) and drape it over a large sieve. Pour the almond milk through the sieve and squeeze out as much liquid as possible. Store the milk in the fridge for a couple of days. Give it a shake before using. You can use the left-over almond pulp in muesli or bread dough, or feed it to your chooks like I do.

Smoothies are wonderful — they pack loads of goodness into one glass.

Gifts from the garden

Beetroot, walnut and pomegranate dip ~ Spiced broad bean and pea dip
Quick pickled baby vegetables ~ Bread and butter pickles ~ Seedy lavosh

This little collection is packed with perfect spring colours, plus loads of flavour.
Easy to transport, eat and keep, any of these dips or pickles would make a beautiful
package with a jar full of seedy crackers. Remember to double the recipes so that
you can also fill your own fridge and pantry shelves.

BEETROOT, WALNUT AND POMEGRANATE DIP

This dip is great with pickled or fresh vegetables and crackers, served alongside barbecued meats, used as a base for a quinoa salad bowl or spread across toasted sourdough and topped with a little feta and rocket (arugula).

4 beetroot (about 700 g/1 lb 9 oz), trimmed
1 Tbsp olive oil, plus extra for drizzling
1 cup (115 g) walnuts, toasted
1 handful dill
Grated zest and juice of 1 lemon
2 Tbsp pomegranate molasses, or to taste
$1/2$ tsp sea salt and a good grinding of black pepper, or to taste
$1/4$ cup (70 g) Greek-style yoghurt

Preheat the oven to 180°C (350°F). Cut the beetroot into quarters, place on a baking tray and drizzle with a little olive oil. Roast for 35 minutes, then tip the walnuts onto another baking tray and add them to the oven for 10 minutes or until they're just turning golden and smelling lovely and aromatic, at which point remove them from the oven. Check that the beetroot is cooked (it'll be tender right through when pierced with a knife) and remove it from the oven as well.

Put the beetroot and walnuts in the bowl of a food processor and add the dill, lemon zest, lemon juice, 1 tablespoon olive oil, pomegranate molasses, salt and pepper. Blitz until you have a smooth-ish purée, then add the yoghurt a little at a time until the dip reaches the desired consistency. Season to taste before serving.

MAKES ABOUT $2^1/2$ CUPS

SPICED BROAD BEAN AND PEA DIP

A deliciously chunky, green dip that's excellent served with crackers and pickles or alongside some grilled fish or chicken. You could also purée this until smooth, thin it out with a nice stock and serve as soup.

2 cups (350 g) broad beans
1 cup (140 g frozen or 160 g fresh) green peas
1 handful coriander (cilantro) leaves
1 handful mint leaves
1 red chilli, finely chopped, or to taste
$1/4$ tsp sea salt
A good pinch of ground cumin
Grated zest and juice of 1 lime
2 Tbsp Greek-style yoghurt

Blanch the broad beans and green peas in boiling water for a few minutes, then drain and refresh under cold water. Double-pod the broad beans if you have time (nobody will really mind if they're only single-podded – the extra step just makes the dip a little smoother and brighter).

Transfer the broad beans and peas to the bowl of a food processor and add the remaining ingredients. Blitz until the dip has a rough consistency. Season to taste, and serve with fresh and/or pickled vegetables and crackers.

MAKES ABOUT $1^1/4$ CUPS

Make a double quantity to keep in
the fridge for emergency snacking.

QUICK PICKLED BABY VEGETABLES

These are also known as 'fridge pickles' or 'the lazy person's pickle', because you don't need to worry about sterilising jars and the like. They are intended to be consumed within a couple of weeks, so they're an easy way to get a little more mileage out of your garden or market haul. Milder and less vinegary than regular pickles, these are especially good made with sweet, pretty baby vegetables. Serve them with dips or a cheese platter, or use them to pep up a simple grain salad.

Enough raw vegetables to fill four 2 cup (500 ml) jars (see Note)
2 cups (500 ml) vinegar (I use 2 parts apple cider vinegar and 1 part white wine vinegar)
¼ cup (55 g) sugar
2 Tbsp sea salt
1 Tbsp coriander seeds, toasted
1 Tbsp yellow mustard seeds
1 Tbsp black peppercorns
1 tsp chilli flakes
1 tsp fennel seeds

Trim your vegetables, slicing any large ones, then pack tightly and prettily into four large jars.

Pour 1½ cups (375 ml) water into a small saucepan and add the vinegar, sugar, salt and spices. Bring to the boil over medium heat.

Carefully pour the hot liquid into the jars, ensuring that the vegetables are completely covered. Seal well and leave on the bench to cool, then store in the fridge for 2–3 weeks. Wait for a day or two before eating the pickles as this will allow the flavours to develop.

MAKES 4 JARS

NOTE
Use any vegetables you like – baby carrots, radishes, beetroot, fennel, green beans, garlic scapes, turnips, zucchini (courgettes), etc. If using cucumber, keep in mind that it has a high water content, so I'd reduce the water by at least ½ cup (125 ml).

BREAD AND BUTTER PICKLES

This recipe is from my mother-in-law, Judith, who enjoys making pickles and delivering them to friends. We are always happy to see lines of pickle jars on her kitchen bench, waiting for us to take home to pile on cheese sandwiches or add to mezze platters with toasted flatbread, yoghurt, olives, tomatoes and feta. Judith adds these pickles to peanut butter sandwiches and serves them alongside barbecued meats, especially our venison.

8 baby Lebanese cucumbers, cut into 6 mm (1/4 inch) slices
2 red onions, thinly sliced
2 tsp salt
1 3/4 cups (435 ml) white wine vinegar
1 cup (220 g) sugar
2 tsp brown mustard seeds
1 tsp fennel seeds
1 tsp coriander seeds

Combine the cucumber, onion and salt in a small bowl and toss well to combine. Cover and place in the fridge overnight (this will soften the cucumber before pickling). The next morning, rinse the cucumber and onion slices and pat dry.

Combine the vinegar, sugar and spices in a small saucepan. Cook over medium heat for 5 minutes, stirring often to dissolve the sugar. Add the sliced cucumber and onion and bring to the boil. Remove from the heat, divide among sterilised jars and seal well. Wait for a couple of days for the flavours to develop before cracking the pickles open.

MAKES ABOUT 3 CUPS

SEEDY LAVOSH

This simple recipe produces gorgeously crisp, flavoursome crackers that are excellent with dips or cheeses. Make up a jar to deliver to a friend, and also keep some in your pantry for snacking at any time of day.

1 1/3 cups (200 g) plain flour
1/3 cup (50 g) sesame seeds
1 tsp fennel seeds
1 tsp nigella seeds
1 tsp sea salt, plus extra for sprinkling
1/4 cup (60 ml) olive oil, plus extra for brushing

Preheat the oven to 170°C (340°F). Grease and line a baking tray with baking paper.

Mix together the flour, seeds and salt in a large bowl. Whisk the olive oil and 1/2 cup (125 ml) water in a small jug, stir into the dry ingredients and work into a rough dough. Turn out onto a work surface and gently knead until soft. Divide the dough into four or five pieces. Roll out one piece of dough between two sheets of baking paper until about 2 mm (1/16 inch) thick. Transfer to the baking tray, brush with a little olive oil and sprinkle with sea salt. Bake the lavosh for 15 minutes or until golden brown, then set aside to cool. Repeat with the remaining dough.

Break the cooled lavosh sheets into shards and store in an airtight container. Alternatively, you can cut the lavosh into neater squares before baking.

VARIATIONS
Instead of (or as well as) the seeds, you could add 1 teaspoon finely chopped fresh or dried rosemary or oregano. A few chilli flakes worked through the dough before baking are good, too.

MAKES ABOUT 20 PIECES

A breakfast picnic is a lovely
friendly way to start the day.

Bring on breakfast

Wholemeal orange and almond muffins ~ Rhubarb compote
Roasted oranges with rosemary and vanilla
Light and crunchy honey granola ~ Spiced coffee

Breakfast often gets overlooked when you're unwell, busy or too stressed to think about anything other than getting well or getting sorted. I'm a big fan of giving someone a basket of breakfast provisions as a gesture of how much you care. It also offers a practical solution to a problem they probably haven't even conceived of yet: that having nothing decent at home for breakfast leads to 'hangriness' (i.e. the angry hunger feelings) by about 11am. In my experience, the 11am hangry pangs tend to lead to bad eating decisions, which lead to feeling even worse and guilty, and so the cycle continues.

Make and pack up these goodies to leave by someone's door or, better yet, organise a breakfast picnic in the golden light of early morning. It's a lovely, friendly way to start the day – and by 9am you've had a good catch-up and you still have the rest of the day ahead of you.

WHOLEMEAL ORANGE AND ALMOND MUFFINS

I'm not usually much of a muffin person. They're often too big, cake-y and sugary for me. But these breakfast muffins are something else entirely – full of flavour and just the right amount of sweetness. Thanks to the roasted almond meal, they stay moist and fresh for longer than a regular muffin. They're delicious served with Rhubarb compote (see below) and a little Greek-style yoghurt.

1 cup (150 g) wholemeal plain flour
½ cup (50 g) almond meal (using freshly roasted, ground almonds makes all the difference)
½ cup (110 g) caster sugar
¼ cup (45 g) soft brown sugar
1½ tsp baking powder
1 egg
150 g (5 oz) butter, melted
100 g (3½ oz) natural Greek-style yoghurt
1 tsp vanilla bean paste
2 oranges, peeled and cut into small chunks

Preheat the oven to 200°C (400°F). Line a 12-hole standard muffin tin with paper cases.

Combine the flour, almond meal, sugars and baking powder in a bowl. Whisk the egg, butter, yoghurt and vanilla together, then gently fold into the dry ingredients until just combined (take care not to over-mix). Fold in the oranges or any extra flavourings (see Variations).

Divide the batter among the muffin cases and bake for 20 minutes or until the muffins are golden on top and firm to touch.

VARIATIONS
Add ½ cup (85 g) chocolate chips and use hazelnut meal instead of almond meal.
Use 1 cup (220 g) poached and roughly chopped pear or quince instead of the oranges.
Replace the oranges with 1 cup (150 g) fresh berries.

MAKES 12

RHUBARB COMPOTE

Preheat the oven to 180°C (350°F). Slice 1 bunch (300 g/10½ oz) trimmed rhubarb into 3 cm (1¼ inch) batons and place in a small roasting tin lined with baking paper. Split 1 vanilla bean lengthways and add it to the tin with the juice of 2 oranges and ⅓ cup (75 g) caster sugar. Toss well, then cover with foil and roast for 25 minutes or until the rhubarb has completely collapsed. **Makes about 2 cups**

ROASTED ORANGES WITH ROSEMARY
AND VANILLA

These roasted oranges are superb with granola and some Greek-style yoghurt. One of my lovely recipe testers commented on the delicious smell that filled the kitchen when she was cooking. Rosemary and citrus are an excellent match, and together make for a comforting, cheerful-smelling kitchen.

4 oranges, peeled and sliced into
   thick rounds
¹/₃ cup (75 g) caster sugar
1 rosemary sprig
1 vanilla bean, split lengthways

Preheat the oven to 180°C (350°F). Line a roasting tin with foil, then top with a sheet of baking paper. Put the oranges on the paper and add the sugar and rosemary. Scrape the vanilla seeds over the oranges and add the vanilla bean. Toss to combine, then wrap up into a tight parcel.

If making this to enjoy now, roast for 25 minutes or until the oranges are soft and fragrant. If making this as a gift, tie the parcel with some twine and add a tag with the cooking instructions.

SERVES 4 (WITH GRANOLA)

LIGHT AND CRUNCHY HONEY GRANOLA

A lovely big bag of home-made granola is one of the best things you can give anyone.
It is, of course, wonderful for breakfast, but it's also good sprinkled over yoghurt and a bit
of fruit at any time of day. This recipe is based on a version I enjoyed one winter morning
in Canberra at the very cool cafe, Mocan and Green Grout. It was served in a beautiful bowl
with warm roasted rhubarb, topped with yoghurt and shards of black sesame praline. You
can add the rhubarb and praline if you like, but I also love it with yoghurt and warm Roasted
oranges with rosemary and vanilla (see opposite).

*¹/₂ cup (175 g) honey (orange
  blossom is good here)*
Grated zest of 1 orange
1 tsp vanilla bean paste
*2 cups (40 g) puffed millet or
  puffed brown rice*
2 cups (200 g) rolled oats
*1 cup (160 g) almonds, roughly
  chopped*
*1 cup (155 g) hazelnuts, skinned
  and roughly chopped*
1 tsp toasted ground cinnamon
¹/₂ tsp ground ginger
A pinch of ground coriander
A pinch of ground cardamom
A pinch of ground cloves
¹/₂ tsp sea salt

Preheat the oven to 150°C (300°F). Line two large baking trays with
baking paper.

Gently warm the honey in a small saucepan over medium–low heat
until runny. Stir in the orange zest and vanilla. Combine the remaining
ingredients in a large bowl, then stir in the warm honey mixture.

Spread the granola over the trays and cook for 40–50 minutes, turning
and tossing the mixture and swapping the trays every 10 minutes until
golden. Turn off the oven and leave the granola in there to cool – this
helps it become crunchy. Store the granola in an airtight container for
up to a couple of weeks.

MAKES 5 CUPS

SPICED COFFEE

Combine 2 cups (175 g) freshly ground coffee (for a plunger) with
2 Tbsp soft brown sugar, ¹/2 tsp ground toasted cardamom (page 75)
and ¹/2 tsp ground ginger in a large heatproof jug. Split ¹/2 vanilla bean
lengthways and add it to the jug, scraping in the seeds. Pour in 3 cups
(750 ml) boiling water and leave to infuse overnight.
    Line a sieve with four layers of muslin (or a couple of clean Chux
cloths) and place over a large bowl. Pour the coffee mixture into the
sieve and discard the coffee grounds. Store the coffee concentrate
in the fridge.
    To serve, heat the coffee concentrate in a small saucepan, then mix
1 part concentrate with 1 part boiling water (or to taste) and add milk
(to taste). **Makes 3 cups (750 ml) concentrate**

Hit the couch

Fennel and sausage ragu ~ Spicy, smoky beef ragu
Just a really good chocolate mousse ~ Blood orange margaritas

These recipes are for when you or your recipient are too sad to do anything more than
sit on the couch, eat something comforting and watch something distracting.
At times like these you need carbs, sausages, a stiff drink, chocolate and
a good line-up of movies or TV shows. I offer up two different but
equally delicious slow-cooked ragu recipes here – take your pick.

Fennel and sausage ragu

FENNEL AND SAUSAGE RAGU

This ragu is all about coaxing the flavour from every ingredient through long, slow cooking. The result is a super-tasty rich sauce to serve over polenta, gnocchi or any kind of pasta. I also use it in my lasagne. If you are making the ragu to give away, bundle it up with some nice pasta, a block of parmesan cheese and a bread stick or, even better, the Garlic bread from page 74.

^{1}/$_3$ cup (80 ml) olive oil
1 red onion, diced
3 garlic cloves, finely chopped
1 tsp fennel seeds
500 g (1 lb 2 oz) really nice Italian sausages (about 4 sausages – a mixture of pork and veal if possible)
200 g (7 oz) pancetta, roughly chopped
1 cup (250 ml) full-bodied red wine
2 x 400 g (14 oz) tins whole tomatoes
^{1}/$_4$ cup (60 g) tomato paste (concentrated purée)
1 cup (250 ml) chicken or vegetable stock

Preheat the oven to 150°C (300°F). Heat the olive oil in a deep ovenproof frying pan or flameproof casserole dish over medium heat. Cook the onion for 5 minutes or until soft and translucent. Add the garlic and fennel seeds and cook for a couple more minutes. Crumble the sausage meat into the pan, discarding the casings. Add the pancetta and increase the heat to medium–high. Cook, stirring often, until the sausage meat and pancetta are browned. Pour in the red wine and let the liquid reduce a little. Now pour in the tomatoes, tomato paste and stock and stir well. Season with salt and pepper to taste.

Clean the side of the pan (any residue may burn and be tricky to wash away). Place in the oven and cook, uncovered, for 3 hours (give it a stir a couple of times). By this point the ragu will have reduced right down.

SERVES 4

SPICY, SMOKY BEEF RAGU

This ragu is layer upon layer of flavour, cooked long and slow in a low oven. It freezes really well and would be great to give someone for a ready meal. I love it with soft polenta and a green salad, but it would also be good with potato mash or even guacamole, tortillas and some pickles.

^{1}/$_3$ cup (80 ml) olive oil
2 onions, finely chopped
4 garlic cloves, finely chopped
1 tsp thyme leaves
2 chorizo sausages, very finely chopped (I give them a whizz in the food processor)
800 g (1 lb 12 oz) chuck steak or other slow-cooking cut, cut into small pieces (your butcher should be happy to do this, otherwise use beef mince)
1 cup (250 ml) full-bodied red wine
2 x 400 g (14 oz) tins whole tomatoes
^{1}/$_3$ cup (90 g) tomato paste (concentrated purée)
4 chipotle chillies in adobo sauce, roughly chopped (you can usually find these in the Mexican section of the supermarket)
1 Tbsp soft brown sugar
1 Tbsp balsamic vinegar
1 tsp salt

Preheat the oven to 140°C (275°F). Heat the oil in a large heavy-based ovenproof saucepan or flameproof casserole dish over medium heat. Add the onion, garlic and thyme and cook, stirring occasionally, for about 10 minutes or until softened.

Add the chorizo, increase the heat to high and cook for a few minutes. Next add the beef and cook for a few more minutes. Pour in the wine and let it bubble down and reduce a little. Add the tomatoes, tomato paste, chillies, sugar, vinegar and salt and stir well.

Transfer to the oven for 4 hours, by which time it will be a rich, deeply flavoured pot of goodness. Stir the ragu every now and then during cooking so that it doesn't stick to the bottom of the pan.

SERVES 6–8

JUST A REALLY GOOD CHOCOLATE MOUSSE

I'm of the belief that a good chocolate mousse can bring a smile to almost any face. So, if you arrive on the doorstep of a sad friend with a bowl of mousse and two spoons, I am fairly confident that the gesture at least will make him or her smile.

This recipe is inspired by a dessert I enjoyed in Paris with my friends Cook and Sasha. We were travelling on a tiny budget, giddy with the fact that we were in Paris and having dinner in a picture–perfect bistro. I will never forget the chocolate mousse that arrived in a huge bowl with three spoons and a jug of cold cream.

The recipe isn't tricky but it does create rather a lot of washing up. The good news is that it's all done well in advance and hopefully forgotten once you start eating. It doubles really well, so why not make two big bowls of mousse – one for your fridge and one for a friend? Transport it in a cool box or chiller bag and store it in the fridge for up to 3 days.

---

100 g (3¹/₂ oz) good-quality milk chocolate
100 g (3¹/₂ oz) good-quality dark chocolate
3 eggs, separated
¹/₂ cup (125 ml) single (pure) cream

If you have an old-school handheld electric beater, now's the time to dig it out. Otherwise, grab an electric mixer with a whisk attachment.

Melt the milk chocolate and dark chocolate together in a glass or ceramic bowl over a saucepan of simmering water, stirring regularly until smooth.

Meanwhile, whisk the egg yolks until pale and fluffy. In another bowl, whip the cream until soft and thick. And in yet another bowl (sorry!), whisk the egg whites until stiff peaks form.

Fold the melted chocolate, a little at a time, into the egg yolks, then fold in the cream and whisk together until smooth (I use a handheld electric mixer here for a quick burst to ensure everything is really well combined). Now very, very gently, fold in the egg whites, a little at a time, until just incorporated. You want to keep as many air bubbles as possible so don't worry if there are still a few streaks of white – I think that's a decent trade-off for such a light mousse. Spoon the mousse into one big bowl or individual glasses and chill for at least 3 hours or for up to 3 days.

SERVES 6

SUGAR SYRUP

Combine ¹/₂ cup (110 g) caster sugar and 1 cup (250 ml) water in a small saucepan. Bring to a simmer and cook, stirring, until the sugar has dissolved. Remove from the heat and set aside to cool. Store in the fridge, ready to use in Blood orange margaritas (see right).
Makes about 1 cup

BLOOD ORANGE MARGARITAS

Cut 1 lime in half, then rub the rims of two glasses with the lime halves. Press the glasses into Lime chilli salt (page 74) or sea salt flakes to coat. Squeeze the lime halves and pour the juice into a cocktail shaker or a jar with 1/2 cup (125 ml) fresh blood orange juice, 1/3 cup (80 ml) sugar syrup, or to taste (see left), 1/3 cup (80 ml) tequila and 1/4 cup (60 ml) Grand Marnier or Cointreau. Add 1 cup (150 g) crushed ice and shake for a good 10 seconds. Pour into the glasses and serve. **Serves 2**

Bring in the big guns

THE chicken pie ~ Syrup-soaked lemon, blueberry and rosemary cake

Drop off a basket containing these goodies and, while it won't unbreak what's broken,
it will at least mean that your friend has a gentle, delicious meal at the ready.
And they'll know that you poured love into it – surely that will part the clouds a little?

THE CHICKEN PIE

I make this pretty much every time I go to cook for someone in need of cheering up. There's something about a golden chicken pie that makes everyone feel good – kids love it, adults do too and it's a whole meal in one.

Yes, this is a labour of love. Yes, you could buy a roast chook and frozen pastry and bung this together in less than half the time and nobody would care. But... there really is something deeply satisfying about making this chicken pie from scratch. And if you do, please take my advice and triple this recipe to make three at once – one to give away, one for your dinner and one for the freezer.

Poaching a whole chicken in aromatics means not only do you get lovely moist chicken and stock to use for the filling and sauce base, but you'll have some chicken and stock left over for sandwiches and soup. Have I convinced you yet?

BASICALLY THERE ARE FOUR PARTS TO THIS PIE:

1. Poach the chicken for chicken meat and stock – 15 minutes hands-on preparation, 1 hour hands-off cooking. (You could substitute a barbecued chicken.)

2. Make the rough puff pastry – 15 minutes hands-on preparation, 50 minutes chilling. (You could use frozen puff pastry instead.)

3. Make the filling – 20 minutes hands-on preparation, 15 minutes cooking.

4. Roll out the pastry, add the filling, assemble and bake – 20 minutes hands-on preparation, 40 minutes cooking.

You don't have to do all of this in one hit. I usually poach the chook and make the filling the day before so it's nice and cool when I put it all together. Then I make the pastry and bake the pie the day I want to deliver or eat it.

One last thing before you get started: I recommend baking this pie in a disposable aluminium pie tin. Not all that beautiful, I know, but they work a treat and mean that your recipient doesn't have to think about washing and returning a dish, which, when you are in need of cheering up, is a bit of a drag.

SERVES 6–8

PART 1:
THE POACHED CHICKEN

1.8 kg (4 lb) whole chicken
2 carrots, roughly chopped
2 celery stalks, roughly chopped
1 onion, roughly chopped
1 tsp black peppercorns
1 tsp sea salt
1 handful parsley (stems and all)
4 thyme sprigs

Wash the chicken and pat dry, then place in a large stockpot, cover with cold water and add the remaining ingredients. Bring to the boil over medium–high heat, watching out for and discarding any scum that comes to the surface (there's a life lesson hidden in a recipe). Reduce the heat and gently simmer for 45 minutes.

Transfer the cooked chicken to a board resting on a tea towel (this will stop any juices dripping onto the bench and the floor). Cover the chicken with a tent of foil and set aside until cool enough to handle.

Return the stockpot to the stovetop and boil until the mixture reduces by about a third – this will take 20 minutes or so and will intensify the flavour. Pour the mixture through a sieve, discarding the aromatics and reserving the stock.

Pull the chicken meat away from the bones and discard the carcass. Cover until needed for the filling or place in the fridge if you're not assembling and baking your pie right away.

PART 2:
THE PASTRY

Rough puff pastry
250 g (9 oz) chilled butter, cut into cubes
1²/₃ cups (250 g) plain flour, plus extra for dusting
¹/₄ cup (60 ml) chilled water

Combine the butter and flour on the bench, using the heel of your hand to work them together. Add water as necessary to form a rough dough – it's okay to see some marbled streaks of butter. Cover with plastic wrap and chill in the fridge for 30 minutes.

On a lightly floured work surface, roll out the pastry until you have a large rectangle. Dust off any loose flour. Fold the top half of the pastry down, then fold the bottom half up so you have a long slim rectangle. Now turn the pastry 90 degrees and roll into another large rectangle, trying to roll in only one direction if possible (this helps keep the butter's 'marbled' effect and ideally will keep your pastry nice and puffy and flaky). Fold and roll again, then cover with plastic wrap and chill for 20 minutes or until needed.

NOTE
If you're using store-bought pastry, I'd recommend shortcrust for the base and puff for the top.

PART 3:
PART 3:
THE FILLING

PART 4:
BRINGING IT ALL TOGETHER

50 g (1 3/4 oz) butter
2 leeks, pale parts only, thinly sliced
2 Tbsp plain flour
2 cups (500 ml) hot chicken stock
1 tsp wholegrain mustard
1 tsp lemon thyme leaves
Grated zest of 1 lemon
150 ml (5 fl oz) single (pure) cream
450 g (3 cups) cooked, shredded chicken

Heat the butter in a large frying pan over medium heat until bubbling. Add the leek, season and cook, stirring often, for 10 minutes. Add the flour and cook, stirring, for a couple of minutes.

Add the hot stock and let it bubble for 2 minutes, stirring often, then stir in the mustard, lemon thyme, lemon zest and cream. Bring back to the boil and cook, stirring often, for a few minutes more, until the sauce thickens up. Taste and season again if needed.

Pop the mixture into the fridge to cool while you roll out the pastry and line the pie tin. When you're ready to assemble the pie, stir in the shredded chicken.

NOTE
It's important that the chicken is only reheated once after it's cooked. If you're making this as a helpful present, assemble the pie but don't bake it – just include a note with the baking instructions.

1 egg
1 Tbsp single (pure) cream

Preheat the oven to 200°C (400°F). Make an egg wash by whisking the egg and cream together.

Roll out the pastry on a lightly floured work surface to a large round, about 3 mm (1/8 inch) thick. Trim the excess pastry, leaving enough to hang over the side of the pie tin, then gently drape the pastry over your rolling pin and unroll it into a pie tin – mine is 22 cm (8 1/2 inches) wide and 4 cm (1 1/2 inches) deep. Press the pastry into the side of the tin, then run the rolling pin over the top to create a clean edge. Roll the excess pastry into a ball and roll it out to a round slightly larger than the top of your pie tin. Cut a small hole in the middle of the pastry (to let steam escape while cooking).

Spoon the chicken filling into the pie tin, brush the pastry edges with a little egg wash and gently press the pastry lid on top. Pop the pie in the fridge for 5 minutes while you do one last (optional) step. Roll out any pastry remains and use some little cutters or a small sharp knife to cut small triangles or whatever pastry shapes you like. Use these shapes to decorate the edge of your pie and cover up any rough bits.

Brush the pastry top with egg wash. Finally, place the pie in the oven and bake for 35–40 minutes or until the pastry is golden brown. Well done, you!

A really great pie can't put the world to rights, but it might at least part the clouds of unhappiness a little.

SYRUP-SOAKED LEMON, BLUEBERRY AND ROSEMARY CAKE

Nothing tricky or fancy here – just the most lovely, simple and soft cake ever. There's something very comforting in its softness and lemony tang. It freezes well, too. One more cheering attribute of this cake: it's a melt-and-mix number so it's super easy to make.

180 g (6 oz) butter, melted
3/4 cup (200 g) plain Greek-style
    yoghurt
Grated zest of 1 lemon
1/4 cup (60 ml) lemon juice
3 eggs, at room temperature
2 cups (300 g) plain flour
1 1/2 cups (330 g) caster sugar
2 tsp baking powder
1 punnet (125 g) blueberries
Rosemary sprigs and flowers,
    to garnish (optional)

Rosemary lemon syrup
1/2 cup (110 g) caster sugar
Grated zest of 2 lemons
1/4 cup (60 ml) lemon juice
2 rosemary sprigs

Preheat the oven to 180°C (350°F). Grease a 24 cm (9 1/2 inch) spring-form cake tin or a bundt tin.

Combine all the ingredients except the blueberries in a food processor or large bowl and either whizz for 10 seconds or stir well by hand until you have a smooth batter. Gently fold in the blueberries.

Pour the batter into the tin and bake for 45 minutes or until the cake is golden brown and just firm to touch. While the cake is baking, prepare the syrup.

For the syrup, combine all the ingredients and 1/4 cup (60 ml) water in a small saucepan. Bring to the boil, then let the mixture bubble away for a few minutes until you have a thick syrup.

As soon as you remove the cake from the oven, poke it all over with a skewer and pour the hot syrup onto the cake. The holes from the skewer will allow the syrup to penetrate right into the cake. Garnish with rosemary sprigs and flowers if you have them.

SERVES 8

This syrup-soaked cake looks
very pretty sprinkled with
rosemary sprigs and flowers.

Two lovely tarts for lunch

Filo, spinach and dill tart ~ Hot-smoked salmon and zucchini tart
Radish and pomegranate salad

Springtime here in Orange means lots of eggs, lots of new greens, and picnic season.
And one of the best things to take and share on a picnic, or give to someone as
an instant meal, is a home-made tart. Plan on delivering these the day you make
them, or freeze them and deliver straight into your friend's freezer or
into their fridge to thaw for lunch or dinner.

FILO, SPINACH AND DILL TART

This simple and easy tart can take all kinds of variations. You could swap silverbeet or kale for the spinach, and add a little cooked chicken or smoked salmon to the ricotta mixture.

¹/₄ cup (60 ml) olive oil
1 red onion, finely diced
8 handfuls English spinach (about 1 big bunch),
roughly chopped, stalks discarded
A few pinches of salt
1 cup (230 g) ricotta cheese
¹/₂ cup (65 g) crumbled feta cheese
4 eggs
Grated zest of 1 lemon
1 handful dill, finely chopped
100 g (3¹/₂ oz) butter, melted
6 sheets filo pastry
²/₃ cup (100 g) pine nuts, toasted
¹/₄ cup (40 g) sesame seeds

Preheat the oven to 220°C (425°F). Heat the olive oil in a frying pan over medium heat and cook the onion for 5 minutes or until soft. Add the spinach, a handful at a time, waiting for it to wilt a little before adding more. Add a few pinches of salt as you go and cook until all of the spinach has just wilted. Remove from the heat and set aside.

Put the ricotta in a large bowl and whisk in the feta, eggs, lemon zest and dill. Season to taste.

Grease a 24 cm (9¹/₂ inch) spring-form cake tin with a little of the melted butter. Lay the pastry out on a work surface. Brush one pastry sheet with the melted butter and gently lay it across the tin, then press into the tin so the excess pastry is hanging over the side. Repeat with the remaining pastry sheets.

Spoon the spinach mixture into the pastry, top with the ricotta mixture and sprinkle with the pine nuts. Bring the pastry edges over the top to make a rough lid. Brush with a little more butter and sprinkle with the sesame seeds. Bake for 35 minutes or until the pastry top is golden brown.

SERVES 6–8

HOT-SMOKED SALMON AND ZUCCHINI TART

Just the loveliest little tart, this one – singing with fresh spring flavour. Once you've prepared the pastry base, it's easy to put together – winning all round!

1 quantity rough puff pastry (page 38)
2 eggs
¹/₂ cup (125 ml) single (pure) cream
¹/₂ cup (50 g) finely grated parmesan cheese
Grated zest of 1 lemon
300 g (10¹/₂ oz) hot-smoked salmon, flaked
1 zucchini (courgette), very thinly sliced

Roll out the pastry on a lightly floured surface until about 5 mm (¹/₄ inch) thick. Drape the pastry over the rolling pin and unroll it into a loose-based fluted tart tin – mine is 20 cm (8 inches) wide and 3 cm (1¹/₄ inches) deep. The pastry will shrink back into the tin when cooking, so minimise this by leaving extra at the top and really pushing the pastry down and into each indent in the side of the tin. Trim the edge, leaving about 5 mm (¹/₄ inch) extra. Return to the fridge for 30 minutes.

Preheat the oven to 200°C (400°F). Prick the pastry base with the tines of a fork. Line with baking paper and fill the base with pastry weights, uncooked rice or dried beans (this stops the base rising during baking). Bake for 10 minutes, then gently remove the weights and baking paper and cook for another 5–10 minutes or until the pastry is just lightly golden and looks dry. Meanwhile, prepare the tart filling.

Whisk together the eggs and cream. Season to taste, then add half of the parmesan and the lemon zest. Pour into the pastry and add the salmon and zucchini. Sprinkle with the remaining parmesan and grind some black pepper over the top. Bake for 25–30 minutes or until the top is golden and just firm to touch.

VARIATIONS
Instead of the zucchini and salmon, you could also use asparagus and goat's curd; caramelised onion and thyme; or roasted pumpkin and beetroot.

SERVES 6–8

The crunchy radish salad works particularly well to offset the rich, creamy salmon tart.

RADISH AND POMEGRANATE SALAD

Cut one telegraph cucumber into chunks, slice a bunch of radishes into thin discs and pick the leaves off a bunch of mint. Combine in a large bowl. Dress with a simple lemon and olive oil dressing and sprinkle with some nigella seeds and pomegranate seeds.
Serves 6

Golden syrup biscuits

An afternoon tea basket

Jam pastries ~ Golden syrup biscuits ~ Vietnamese iced coffee ~ Dot's sponge

This is the kind of afternoon tea basket that will keep helpers
happy on a working bee, bring a sweet note to a tricky gathering
or just make someone feel extra loved and looked after.

JAM PASTRIES

Few home-made treats are more appreciated than a batch of warm pastries filled with jam or vanilla custard. They do, I concede, require terrifying amounts of butter, but... needs must! Fill them with jam as I've done here, or with custard, a layer of frangipane and some thin slices of poached pear or apple. Or try apple and custard, sprinkled with some slivered almonds. Fresh berries are also delicious.

The pastries are best on the day they're made, but can be reheated the next day. If you're freezing them, pop them in the oven straight from the freezer to reheat.

1 Tbsp (15 g) dried yeast
150 ml (5 fl oz) lukewarm water
A pinch of salt
2 Tbsp caster sugar, plus extra for sprinkling
1 egg
350 g (2¹/₃ cups) plain flour, plus extra for dusting
320 g (11¹/₄ oz) chilled unsalted butter, cut into thin strips
¹/₂ cup (165 g) jam (quince is particularly good)

Egg wash
1 egg
2 Tbsp single (pure) cream

Mix the yeast with the water. Add the salt, sugar and egg and, using your hand shaped like a claw, bring everything together into a lovely shaggy mess. Add the flour and turn the mixture out onto a lightly floured surface. Knead until smooth and elastic, about 5 minutes. Place the dough in a lightly oiled bowl, cover with plastic wrap and leave it to rest in the fridge for 30 minutes.

Roll out the dough on a lightly floured surface into a large rectangle, about 40 x 30 cm (16 x 12 inches). Arrange all of the butter in the centre. (I know it looks like a lot, and it is, but it's worth it.) Fold the dough edges over the butter to meet in the middle, as if you're making a dough envelope.

Turn the dough over so the seam is sitting underneath, then gently roll into a 40 x 30 cm (16 x 12 inch) rectangle again. Fold a third of the dough into the centre, then fold the other third over the top so that you have three layers of dough. Wrap in plastic and pop back in the fridge for 20 minutes. Take out, reroll and return to the fridge for another 20 minutes. Repeat the rolling and chilling once more.

Line a large baking tray with baking paper. Gently roll out the pastry into a 48 x 36 cm (19 x 4¹/₄ inch) rectangle and cut this into 12 cm (4¹/₂ inch) squares. Place a dollop of jam in the centre of one pastry square, fold the edges over to make a little parcel and place on the tray. Repeat with the remaining pastry squares. Let the pastries rest in a warm place for 20 minutes. Meanwhile, preheat the oven to 220°C (425°F).

Whisk the egg and cream together to make an egg wash. Brush over the pastries, sprinkle with a little extra sugar and bake for 15 minutes or until golden brown.

MAKES 12

GOLDEN SYRUP BISCUITS

When I make these biscuits, I feel happy and loved. The taste and smell catapult me back to my Gran's old kitchen in the Blue Mountains. I hope you find them as deliciously comforting as I do.

200 g (7 oz) unsalted butter, softened
1 cup (220 g) caster sugar
2 Tbsp golden syrup
1 tsp vanilla bean paste
2 cups (300 g) plain flour
1 tsp baking powder
A pinch of salt

Preheat the oven to 180°C (350°F). Grease and line two baking trays with baking paper.

Using an electric mixer with a paddle attachment (or a wooden spoon and a strong arm), cream the butter, sugar, golden syrup and vanilla until pale and fluffy.

Sift the flour, baking powder and salt together, then add to the butter mixture. Tip the mixture out onto a work surface and bring together until just combined.

Split the dough into six balls. Roll and squeeze each ball into a sausage shape, about a thumb's width and around 16 cm (6¼ inches) long. Place on the baking trays and bake for 15 minutes or until golden and slightly risen. They will flatten and spread out quite a bit – don't worry! Remove from the oven and cool for a few minutes before cutting into biscuits about 4 cm (1½ inches) wide.

MAKES ABOUT 30

VIETNAMESE ICED COFFEE

Combine 1 cup (250 ml) strong filter coffee, 1 cup (135 g) ice cubes and 1 Tbsp sweetened condensed milk in a large jar. Screw the lid on tightly and give everything a good shake. Serve immediately or shake again before serving. **Serves 2**

DOT'S SPONGE

The best sponge ever! Fluffy, light and just so delicious – big thanks to Dot Yeatman and the team at the Manildra flour mill in central western New South Wales for this recipe.

This cake is bound to cheer and please. Make it for your favourite birthday person, a work afternoon tea, or to enter in your local show. I've doubled Dot's recipe to make a nice tall layer cake, but if you'd prefer something a little smaller or just one layer, then halve away.

8 eggs, separated
1½ cups (330 g) caster sugar
²/₃ cup (100 g) self-raising flour
1 cup (125 g) cornflour
1 cup (250 ml) Lemon and passionfruit curd (page 75)
300 ml (10½ fl oz) single (pure) cream, whipped
250 g (9 oz) strawberries, sliced
4 passionfruit

Preheat the oven to 180°C (350°F). Grease and line two 20 cm (8 inch) spring-form cake tins with baking paper.

Whisk the egg whites to a stiff froth. Gradually add the sugar and beat until thick and smooth. Whisk in the egg yolks, one at a time. Sift the flours together three times. Fold into the egg and sugar mixture with an upward and over movement (do not stir).

Pour half the batter into each cake tin and bake for 20–25 minutes or until the cakes are just firm to touch. Set aside for 5 minutes before turning out onto a wire rack to cool.

Spread the lemon curd over one cake and top with some of the whipped cream, then top with the second cake. Decorate with the remaining cream, strawberries and passionfruit pulp.

MAKES ONE 20 CM (8 INCH) CAKE

Spring picnic hamper

Caramelised onion butter ~ Chicken sandwich mix with a wholegrain loaf
Garlic scape and zucchini fritters ~ Swirly, crunchy rocky road

Spring is the perfect time for country picnics. The snakes aren't awake yet
(or shouldn't be), the flies aren't out in force yet (or shouldn't be) and it's not too
hot to throw out a rug and spend an afternoon with friends, feasting in the sun.
This menu makes a really lovely spring picnic but it could just as easily be
packaged up and given to a lucky friend.

Caramelised onion butter with radishes

CARAMELISED ONION BUTTER

I adore this richly flavoured butter. It's delicious with fresh, peppery radishes, but also pretty special served with a perfectly barbecued steak or stuffed into a roast potato and topped with chives and/or rocket (arugula) leaves.

¼ cup (60 ml) olive oil
3 onions, diced
1 tsp fennel seeds
150 g (5½ oz) unsalted butter, softened
Smoked sea salt, to taste (see Note)

Heat the oil in a frying pan over medium–low heat, add the onion and cook for 15 minutes or until soft and caramelised. Transfer the onion to a bowl to cool.

Wipe out the frying pan and toss in the fennel seeds, then return to the heat and toast for a few minutes or until fragrant. Add the fennel seeds to the bowl with the onion.

Once the onion has cooled, add the butter and salt and stir until well combined. Pack the butter into a bowl or roll it into a log, wrap in baking paper and place in the fridge to firm up.

NOTE
Smoked sea salt is easy to find in most delicatessens. You could, of course, just use regular sea salt and it would still be delicious – the smoked version just adds a little extra oomph.

MAKES ABOUT ½ CUP

Double this recipe and keep a batch in the freezer for flavour emergencies.

CHICKEN SANDWICH MIX WITH A WHOLEGRAIN LOAF

Chicken sandwiches make a simple but very tasty picnic lunch, and they are also great for school lunches. You can either make up the sandwiches or present them in parts as I have done here – the mix and the sliced bread can be frozen. Take care to keep the chicken mixture cool while in transit – a cool box or chiller bag and an ice brick will do the trick.

Many friends have also told me that chicken sandwiches stand out as the most useful, tasty offering they have been gifted during difficult times. One friend told me that after her father passed away, a neighbour came around with a tray of tightly wrapped chicken sandwiches and put them straight in the freezer. A few nights later, the family, completely exhausted after the funeral, collapsed on the couch with a few beers and the thawed chicken sandwiches. She said it was one of the most welcome meals of her life.

Shredded meat from 1 whole poached chicken or purchased barbecued chicken (see Note)
¾ cup (185 g) good-quality mayonnaise
½ cup (80 g) pine nuts, toasted
3 celery stalks, diced
1 handful dill, finely chopped
Juice of 1 lemon
2 Tbsp dijon mustard
1–2 loaves fresh, sliced wholegrain bread

Mix the shredded chicken with the mayonnaise, pine nuts, celery, dill, lemon juice and mustard. Season to taste. Serve with the sliced bread.

NOTE
You'll need about 3 cups (450 g) of shredded cooked chicken. I like to poach a whole chicken following the instructions in the chicken pie recipe (page 38) – this is cheaper and yields more delicious chicken, but there's nothing wrong with using a barbecued chook.

MAKES ABOUT 8 SANDWICHES OR 24 FINGER SANDWICHES

GARLIC SCAPE AND ZUCCHINI FRITTERS

Garlic scapes appear in our farmers' markets in spring, right before the garlic harvest. They are long, curly shoots with a punchy, peppery garlic flavour. They're gorgeous stir-fried, pounded into pesto or sliced and fried up in these tasty little fritters. These are ideal picnic or basket fare, great at room temperature or straight from the pan. If you can't lay your hands on garlic scapes, spring onions mixed with a couple of finely chopped garlic cloves would work beautifully too.

3 zucchini (courgettes), grated
$^1\!/_2$ tsp salt
1 bunch garlic scapes (about 8), trimmed
   and finely chopped
$^1\!/_2$ cup (115 g) ricotta cheese
2 eggs
1 tsp grated lemon zest
$^3\!/_4$ cup (110 g) self-raising flour
Olive oil, for frying

Minted yoghurt
1 cup (260 g) plain yoghurt
1 handful mint leaves, finely chopped
Juice of 1 lemon
Chilli flakes (optional)

Combine the grated zucchini and salt in a small bowl. Transfer the mixture to a colander and set it above the bowl. Leave to drain for 30 minutes.

Meanwhile, for the minted yoghurt, mix the yoghurt, mint and lemon juice together. Season to taste, and top with a few chilli flakes if you like it hot. Cover and chill while you prepare the fritters.

Combine the drained zucchini with the garlic scapes, ricotta, eggs and lemon zest in a bowl and mix well. Fold in the flour and season to taste.

Heat a tablespoon or so of olive oil in a frying pan over medium–high heat. Dollop a tablespoon of the batter into the pan and then add two more dollops so you are cooking three fritters at once, for about a minute on each side or until golden brown. Transfer to a plate lined with paper towel. Repeat with the remaining batter, then serve warm or at room temperature with the minted yoghurt.

MAKES ABOUT 12–15

SWIRLY, CRUNCHY ROCKY ROAD

Rocky road always goes down well and this one, I promise, will be a particular crowd pleaser. I love the salted peanuts, and the ginger works well for me, but you can of course swap in or out anything you prefer. Try adding half a cup of broken shortbread biscuits, or perhaps some jellies or dried cranberries.

1 ⅓ cups (200 g) roughly chopped good-quality
    dark chocolate
1 ⅓ cups (200 g) roughly chopped good-quality
    white chocolate
1 cup (90 g) nice marshmallows, cut into pieces
    with scissors
¾ cup (110 g) salted peanuts
½ cup (110 g) crystallised ginger
Edible flowers, to decorate

Grease and line a 20 cm (8 inch) square cake tin with baking paper. Melt the dark chocolate in a bowl over a saucepan of simmering water. Do the same with the white chocolate, in a separate bowl.

Stir the marshmallows, peanuts and ginger into the dark chocolate. Spoon the mixture into the tin and swirl in the white chocolate, using a knife to mix. Sprinkle with a few edible flowers for decoration, then place in the fridge to set for at least 2 hours.

Once hardened, cut the rocky road into pieces and package up for your lucky friends. If the weather's warm, store it in the fridge.

MAKES ABOUT 20 PIECES

Spring drinks to bottle

St Joseph's lemonade ~ Elderflower cordial ~ Elderflower vodka ~ Strawberry and elderflower pops

I like to prepare ahead for the Christmas season and stock the pantry with beautiful bottles of home-made drinks. It means I always have something a bit special at the ready, either to give as a gift or to enjoy with friends.

ST JOSEPH'S LEMONADE

This recipe comes via St Joseph's school in Molong, New South Wales. The kids there made a big batch of lemonade to sell and raise funds for their kitchen garden, which I visited and wrote about for my blog. It's a great simple recipe and extra easy when you have lots of little hands to help squeeze all those lemons!

800 ml (28 fl oz) freshly squeezed lemon juice
Zest of 2 lemons (slice thin strips of the skin, so it is easy to remove later)
2 kg (4 lb 8 oz) sugar
3 tsp citric acid

Pour 2.4 litres (84 fl oz) water into a large saucepan. Add the lemon juice and lemon zest and bring to the boil. Pour in the sugar, stirring until it has dissolved. Take the pan off the heat and stir in the citric acid. Allow to cool, then discard the lemon zest.

Strain the lemon juice and divide among sterilised bottles. Seal and store in the fridge.

MAKES 4 LITRES OR JUST OVER FIVE 3 CUP (750 ML) BOTTLES

Dilute the lemonade mix with cold water and serve with lots of ice.

ELDERFLOWER CORDIAL

20 elderflower heads
4 lemons
2¼ cups (500 g) caster sugar

Wash the elderflower well. Juice one of the lemons; thinly slice the rest.

Combine the sugar and 4 cups (1 litre) water in a large non-reactive saucepan and bring to the boil, stirring until the sugar has dissolved. Remove the pan from the heat. Add the lemon juice, lemon slices and elderflower. Cover the pan and set aside for 24 hours.

Strain the liquid, discarding the flowers and lemon slices. Decant the cordial into sterilised jars ready to be given away or stored in your fridge.

MAKES 4 CUPS (1 LITRE)

There's something quite special about the creamy, lemony, floral aroma of elderflower. It grows wild along the creek on our farm and seems to pop up along roadsides and in gardens all over the country. Apparently one must endeavour to pick elderflower only on sunny days, only picking the flower heads that are facing the sun. Or so they say.

I love elderflower cordial with lots of sparkling water and ice, but it's also gorgeous with prosecco or vodka and soda, and makes a lovely jelly or sorbet base. The elderflower vodka is also lovely with sparkling water over crushed ice.

ELDERFLOWER VODKA

10 elderflower heads
1 cup (220 g) sugar
Grated zest and juice of 1 lemon
4 cups (1 litre) vodka

Pick through the flowers to make sure there aren't any bugs or other nasties in there, then pack them into a large jar. Add the sugar, lemon zest, lemon juice and vodka, then seal and give it a good shake. Leave in a dark place to infuse for one month.

Line a strainer with muslin and strain the vodka into a clean bottle. The vodka will be delicious to drink now, but will develop a more full-bodied flavour after a month or two.

MAKES 4 CUPS (1 LITRE)

STRAWBERRY AND ELDERFLOWER POPS

Blend 250 g (9 oz) strawberries with 1 cup (250 ml) elderflower cordial and 2 cups (500 ml) water. Check the taste. The flavour will dull a little when frozen, so you might want to make it sweeter than you would make it to drink by adding more cordial. If it's too sweet, add a little more water or puréed strawberries. Pour into 8 ice-block moulds (if you don't have them, ice-cube trays will do the trick). Freeze for at least 4 hours or until frozen solid. **Makes 8**

Sweet pickles parcel

Sweet verjus-pickled rhubarb with bay ~ Sweet verjus-pickled strawberries with vanilla and pink peppercorns
Orange and quinoa biscuits

These sweet pickles make a lovely care package for a friend in need of a bit of extra love.
Sweet pickles are a gorgeous way to semi-preserve soft spring berries and such. These
recipes are 'fresh pickles', meaning they aren't made to last for months, just a week or
so, and need to be kept in the fridge. They are beautiful served with goat's curd and
the not-too-sweet orange and quinoa biscuits, but also fantastic with harder,
stronger cheeses or even over ice cream or a simple almond cake or cheesecake.
Verjus is the perfect pickling agent to use here. The acid is softer than vinegar
or lemon juice, yet enough to cut through the fruit's sweetness.

SWEET VERJUS-PICKLED RHUBARB WITH BAY

1 bunch or 300 g (10¹/2 oz) trimmed rhubarb,
 cut into 2 cm (³/4 inch) pieces
³/4 cup (185 ml) verjus
¹/2 cup (110 g) caster sugar
1 vanilla bean, split lengthways
Zest of 1 lemon, cut into thick strips
3 bay leaves

Pack the rhubarb into a large jar. Combine ¹/2 cup (125 ml) water with the verjus, sugar, vanilla bean, lemon zest and bay leaves in a small saucepan. Bring to the boil, stirring occasionally, then remove from the heat and set aside to cool for 10 minutes.

Pour the mixture over the rhubarb, seal and store in the fridge for up to a week.

MAKES 1 LARGE JAR

SWEET VERJUS-PICKLED STRAWBERRIES WITH VANILLA AND PINK PEPPERCORNS

500 g (1 lb 2 oz) strawberries,
 hulled and halved
³/4 cup (185 ml) verjus
¹/2 cup (110 g) caster sugar
1 vanilla bean, split lengthways
Zest of 1 orange, cut into thick strips
1 tsp pink peppercorns

Pack the strawberries into a large jar. Combine ¹/2 cup (125 ml) water with the verjus, sugar, vanilla bean, orange zest and pink peppercorns in a small saucepan. Bring to the boil, stirring occasionally, then remove from the heat and set aside to cool for 10 minutes.

Pour the mixture over the strawberries, seal and store in the fridge for up to a week.

MAKES 1 LARGE JAR

ORANGE AND QUINOA BISCUITS

Dead easy to make, these taste beautiful and pack loads of crunch. Plus, they last for ages in the biscuit tin and are perfect spread with goat's curd and topped with either of the sweet pickle concoctions. They also make a great base for ice cream sandwiches.

50 g (1³/4 oz) butter, melted
1¹/3 cups (125 g) quinoa flakes
1 cup (220 g) caster sugar
2 eggs, lightly beaten
2 Tbsp plain flour
2 tsp baking powder
A pinch of salt
Grated zest of 1 orange

Preheat the oven to 180°C (350°F). Line two baking trays with baking paper.

Mix the melted butter with the quinoa flakes, sugar and eggs. Sift in the flour, baking powder and salt, add the orange zest and gently mix together.

Drop small amounts of the mixture onto the trays (about a teaspoon for each biscuit). Leave plenty of space for the mixture to spread – at least 5 cm (2 inches) between each one. (I usually make only six biscuits per tray.) Bake for 12 minutes or until golden. Leave on the tray to cool for a few minutes before transferring to a wire rack to cool completely.

MAKES ABOUT 20

Chilly spring evening supper

Baked ricotta with spring greens ~ Nutty sweet potato and lime soup

Spring can mess with your head and wardrobe, don't you think? Just when I think it's warming up and put away the warm blankets and woollies, the weather turns cool again. This basket of goodness is for those chilly spring nights. Get a few friends together, set the kitchen bench with a jar of pretty spring flowers and catch up over a bowl of soup and a beautiful baked ricotta. Or pack this up and deliver it to someone in need of some soothing soup and a friend. Add the Chocolate mousse from page 34 for extra brownie points.

BAKED RICOTTA WITH SPRING GREENS

Baked ricotta is something I make constantly, always the same basic recipe, topped with whatever might be in season or just baked as it is. It's beautiful served warm or at room temperature, in wedges or small cubes with drinks, even sliced and sandwiched between warm slices of sourdough toast. It's also great to make and give away as it keeps quite nicely for a few days and makes a change from the good old frittata.

2 cups (460 g) ricotta cheese
1 cup (95 g) grated parmesan cheese, plus extra for sprinkling
5 eggs (lovely big free-range ones)
1 tsp thyme leaves
2 handfuls spring greens – I've used broad beans, baby leeks sliced into thin strips, some roughly chopped new season garlic and a few chopped asparagus spears

Preheat the oven to 180°C (350°F). Grease and line a cake tin, roughly 28 x 22 cm (11¼ x 8½ inches), with baking paper (or grease well).

Whisk the ricotta, parmesan, eggs and thyme, and season with salt and pepper.

Spoon the mixture into the tin. Top with the spring greens and a little extra parmesan, then pop into the oven for about 25 minutes or until golden brown and just firm to touch. Serve warm or at room temperature. Lovely with a good home-made chutney.

SERVES 4–6

NUTTY SWEET POTATO AND LIME SOUP

With the soothing heft of sweet potato and a lighter note thanks to the lime and lime leaves, this is a gorgeous soup and just the thing for a cool spring dinner.

2 Tbsp extra virgin olive oil
1 brown onion, finely diced
750 g (1 lb 10 oz) sweet potato, peeled and cut into 4 cm (1½ inch) chunks
4 cm (1½ inch) piece ginger, peeled and roughly chopped
2½ cups (625 ml) chicken or vegetable stock
6–8 kaffir lime leaves
⅓ cup (90 g) nice natural peanut butter
1 tsp soft brown sugar
Juice of 2 limes, plus extra to serve
1 cup (250 ml) coconut milk

Heat the olive oil in a large saucepan over medium–high heat. Cook the onion for a few minutes until soft and translucent. Add the sweet potato and ginger and cook for a few more minutes, then pour in the stock and bring to the boil.

Scrunch the lime leaves in your palm to release the flavour, then add to the pan and reduce the heat to a simmer. Cook for about 20 minutes or until the sweet potato is tender. Discard the lime leaves.

Blend the soup with the peanut butter and brown sugar until smooth. Stir in the lime juice and enough coconut milk to bring the soup to the desired thickness. Check the seasoning, adding a little more lime juice, salt or a touch of sugar to get that lovely balance of sweet, salty and sour. Serve with extra lime juice.

SERVES 4–6

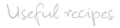
GARLIC BREAD

3 garlic cloves, peeled
100 g (3¹/₂ oz) butter, softened
1 handful flat-leaf parsley, finely chopped
¹/₄ cup (25 g) finely grated parmesan cheese
1 baguette or loaf of nice bread

Combine the garlic, butter, parsley and parmesan with some salt and pepper in a food processor and whizz to combine, or place in a mortar and bash around with the pestle until combined.

Cut the bread into 3 cm (1¹/₄ inch) slices, without cutting all the way through. Spread a little garlic butter on each slice, then spread any extra over the top of the baguette.

Tightly wrap the baguette in foil and keep in the fridge until ready to bake. When that time comes, preheat the oven to 200°C (400°F). Cook the wrapped baguette for 30 minutes, then open up the foil so the top of the baguette is exposed and cook it for another 15 minutes or until golden. Serve warm.

NOTE
The garlic bread can be prepared and left in the fridge, wrapped with foil and ready to be baked, for up to 4 days.

SERVES 4–6

LIME CHILLI SALT

Zest of 2 limes, peeled off in strips
1 bird's eye chilli, chopped
1 cup (225 g) sea salt flakes (pink if you can find them)

Preheat the oven to 140°C (275°F). Line a baking tray with baking paper. Put the lime zest on one half of the tray and chilli on the other. Cook for 20 minutes or until dried and beginning to curl up around the edges.

Using a spice grinder or mortar and pestle, finely chop or pound the lime zest, and then the chilli. Mix the lime zest and chilli with the sea salt and store in a jar.

NOTE
This chilli salt is wonderful with juicy watermelon, as well as pan-fried fish, barbecued chicken or sliced peaches. It also makes a worthwhile hangover helper when sprinkled on peanut butter toast with an extra squeeze of lime!

MAKES ABOUT 1 CUP

GROUND TOASTED CARDAMOM

⅓ cup (35 g) cardamom pods

Preheat the oven to 140°C (275°F). Scatter the cardamom pods over a baking tray and bake for 10 minutes or until beginning to turn dark green. Cool, then transfer to a high-powered blender, food processor, spice grinder or coffee grinder and blitz as finely as possible. Pass through a sieve to remove any larger pieces.

Store in an airtight container as the best ground cardamom ever.

MAKES ABOUT 1½ TABLESPOONS

LEMON AND PASSIONFRUIT CURD

220 g (7¾ oz) unsalted butter
1⅔ cups (370 g) caster sugar
Grated zest and juice of 4 lemons – you need ¾ cup (185 ml) juice
6 eggs, lightly beaten
½ cup (125 g) passionfruit pulp (you'll need about 4 passionfruit)

Put the butter, sugar and lemon zest in a glass bowl resting over a saucepan of simmering water. Cook, stirring often, for about 5 minutes until the butter has melted and the sugar has dissolved.

Add the eggs, lemon juice and passionfruit pulp and cook, gently whisking, for 20 minutes or until the mixture has thickened and coats the back of a wooden spoon – if you have a sugar thermometer, setting point will be around 80°C (176°F). Spoon into clean jars, seal and keep in the fridge for up to 2 weeks.

NOTE
If you prefer to make just lemon curd, leave out the passionfruit and add one more lemon.

MAKES ABOUT 5 CUPS

ACKNOWLEDGEMENTS

This book is for Tim, Alice and Tom. Our little family is everything to me. Thank you, guys, for your love and support, and, right back at you.

As anyone whose primary income depends on primary industry knows, the farming life can be really hard. It's a juggle, a gamble and a 24 hour/7 days a week job. And yes, it's a cliche, but despite the challenges we do look around us every day and feel grateful we get to live here on this farm, in this place together. Thank you, Tim and ALL of the farmers who grow and produce our food, for keeping the boat afloat through drought, bushfires, all the uncertainties and challenges.

Thank you to my parents, Annie and Henry Herron, whose beautiful property features prominently throughout this book. Thank you for giving my siblings and me confidence, opportunity and a home we always love to come back to.

Thank you to the team at Murdoch Books, especially Corinne Roberts who has guided me through this process with such skill and warmth, and designer Vivien Valk who has worked so hard to make this book so beautiful.

Big thanks to Josie Chapman for opening up her beautiful cottages at the Old Convent B&B Borenore for some of the photography.

Making and sharing good, simple, seasonal food is an act of love and generosity, so my final thanks is to you, for buying this book and hopefully taking inspiration from it to go out and leave a basket of home-made food at someone's door soon. It will mean so much to them.

INDEX

This edition published in 2020 by Murdoch Books, an
imprint of Allen & Unwin
Content originally published in *A Basket by the Door*,
published in 2019 by Murdoch Books

Murdoch Books UK
Ormond House, 26–27 Boswell Street,
London, WC1N 3JZ
Phone: +44 (0) 20 8785 5995
murdochbooks.co.uk
info@murdochbooks.co.uk

For corporate orders & custom publishing
contact our business development team at
salesenquiries@murdochbooks.com.au

Publisher: Corinne Roberts
Cover design: northwoodgreen.com
Internal design: Vivien Valk
Editor: Justine Harding
Production director: Lou Playfair

Photography: Sophie Hansen, except page 2
by Clancy Paine

ISBN 978 1 911 63279 5

A catalogue record for this book is available from the
British Library

Printed by C&C Offset Printing Co Ltd, China

TABLESPOONS: We have used Australian 20 ml
(4 teaspoon) tablespoon measures. If you are using a
smaller European 15 ml (3 teaspoon) tablespoon, add
an extra teaspoon of the ingredient for each tablespoon
specified in the recipe.

10 9 8 7 6 5 4 3 2 1